MW01268140

Eating Disorders

Jenny Bryan

RSVP

**RAINTREE
STECK-VAUGHN**
P U B L I S H E R S
A Steck-Vaughn Company

Austin, Texas

www.steck-vaughn.com

Published by Raintree Steck-Vaughn Publishers, an imprint of Steck-Vaughn Company

Library of Congress Cataloging-in-Publication Data
Bryan, Jenny.
Eating disorders / Jenny Bryan.
    p.   cm.—(Talking points)
    Includes bibliographical references and index.
    Summary: Investigates several different kinds of eating disorders, including anorexia, bulimia, and compulsive eating, explaining their symptoms and how society may play a part in both promoting and stopping them.
    ISBN 0-8172-5321-1
    1. Eating disorders—Juvenile literature.
    [1. eating disorders.]
    I. Title. II. Series: Talking points.
    RC552.E18B77 1999
    616.85'26—dc21   99-23147

Printed in Italy. Bound in the United States.
1 2 3 4 5 6 7 8 9 0 04 03 02 01 00

Picture acknowledgments
John Birdsall 4, 37, 43, 44; Bubbles Photo Library, *cover*, 22, 24 (Pauline Cutler), 26 (Dr. Hercules Robinson), 28 (Pauline Cutler), 33 (Pauline Cutler), 40 (Ian West), 45 (Loisjoy Thurston), 54 (Pauline Cutler); Mary Evans Picture Library 5, 17; Format Photographers 25 (Jenny Matthews), 27 (Jenny Matthews), 55, 59 (Sacha Lehrfreund); Sally and Richard Greenhill 7; Angela Hampton Family Life Pictures 8, 30t, 31, 32, 46, 51b, 58; Impact Photos Ltd. 29 (Louise Oligny), 35 (Gary Parker), 36 (Louise Oligny), 42 (Brian Rybolt), 50 (Bruce Stephens); Panos Pictures 6 (Christine Stowers), 51t, 52 (Ron Gilling), 53 (Penny Tweedie); Photofusion 41 (Clarissa Leahy); Popperfoto 11, 13 (John Sholtis), 14 (Paolo Cocco), 15 (Gareth Watkins), 18, 19, 20, 21 (Peter Morgan), 38 (Andre Camara), 56; Retna Pictures Ltd 10 (John Powell), 47 (John Powell), 49 (Philip Reeson), 57 (Bill Davila); Science Photo Library 9 (John Bavosi), 23, 30b (Ed Young), 39 (Sheila Terry); Wayland Picture Library 16.

Contents

What are eating disorders?   4

The body beautiful?   14

Anorexia   23

Bulimia   33

Compulsive eating   39

Dieting and obesity   43

The future   53

Glossary   60

Books to read   62

Useful addresses   63

Index   64

What are eating disorders?

Food is vital to all life on Earth. Without it, we die—although not right away. Human beings can live for only a few days without water, especially if the weather is very hot. But we can live for weeks with little or no food. Most people eat about as much as their body needs to work properly. However, those with eating disorders eat far less or far more than they need to live normally.

There is still debate among nutrition experts about what a "healthy" diet is, and studies continue to investigate the advantages and disadvantages of fat, sugar, and fiber.

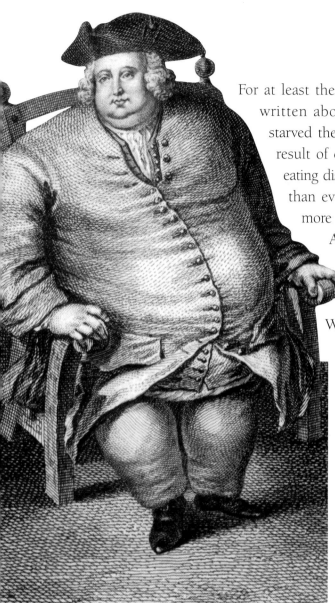

For at least the last 300 years, doctors have written about people who deliberately starved themselves to death or died as a result of overeating. But more cases of eating disorders are being reported now than ever before, and they are much more widespread around the world. At least 2 million people in the United States are affected; in the UK at least 250,000.

Why should this be? What is it about modern living that is making so many people—most of them young—eat in a way that can make them ill, do permanent damage to their bodies, or even kill them?

Edward Bright, of Maldon, Essex, in England. The fact that he was very overweight probably contributed to his early death in 1750, at the age of 30.

Voluntary starvation

"She began to abstain from all solid food ... as also from all other sorts both of meat and drinks, except now and then a few drops of syrup and stew'd prunes, water and sugar, or the juice of a roasted raisin, but these repasts are used so seldom, and in such small quantities as are prodigiously insufficient for sustenation ... and though her upper parts be less emaciated (though too much) yet her lower parts are very languid and inept for motion ...."

John Reynolds, physician and minister, *A Discourse on Prodigious Abstinence*, 1669

Types of eating disorders

At one time, eating disorders were limited mainly to those living in richer countries, such as North America, Europe, and Australia. However, in the last few years, eating disorders have been reported in many cultures where people are exposed to the "western" diet. Orientals, Asians, and Afro-Caribbeans who have settled in Europe and the United States are particularly at risk. This is because their lifestyles become gradually more westernized, and this can lead to conflicting cultural pressures. These are felt most by the young, some of whom can develop eating disorders as a result.

When families move to Europe and America they take on western eating habits and soon become prone to western diseases.

There are three main types of eating disorders. People with anorexia nervosa (usually called anorexia) eat very little because they are afraid of gaining weight. As a result they lose large amounts of weight and become very thin. However, they still believe that they are too fat and refuse to eat properly. Those with bulimia nervosa (usually called bulimia) eat large amounts of food in a short period of time and then vomit the food because they believe this will stop them from gaining weight.

Finally, compulsive eating of large amounts of food, often by people who are already overweight, is also an eating disorder and leads to further weight gain. Compulsive eaters often alternate between overeating and dieting to try to lose the extra weight and have difficulty establishing a normal, healthy way of eating.

Even when they are very ill, people with anorexia may pretend there is nothing wrong and resist efforts to help them.

Why we need food

We need food as fuel for the body, much as a vehicle needs gasoline. After it is broken down in the stomach and intestine, our fuel is carried in the bloodstream, as glucose, to cells all over the body. Here it is further broken down to provide energy for thousands of biochemical (also called metabolic) reactions, which take place every second of the waking and sleeping day. These reactions allow us to think, speak, breathe, move, and do all the things we take for granted as healthy human beings. Some glucose is converted to a chemical called glycogen, which is stored in our muscles and liver for later use.

Food gives us the energy to lead active, healthy lives.

If we eat too little there will not be enough energy to keep the body working. Systems start to break down; people feel tired and move more slowly. Without enough food to process, digestion becomes faulty. People get infections and their immune systems cannot fight them off.

When the walls of the arteries are damaged by fatty deposits it is easy for blood cells to stick to the surface and form clots that eventually cause a blockage.

Taking in more food than we are able to burn off can also be dangerous but it takes longer to see the effects. If we constantly consume more energy than we need, it builds up as fat around the body. Some fat is visible, for example, around the waist, hips, and thighs. But it is the fat we cannot see that is most dangerous.

This builds up on the walls of important blood vessels, such as those to the heart and the brain. In the end, these can become blocked and lead to a heart attack or stroke. Either of these can kill. People who are very overweight also have breathing and movement problems. Their arms and legs simply cannot take the strain of carrying around so much excess fat.

Talking point

"On a planet where millions die of starvation or the complications of malnutrition each year, it is a tragic paradox that in some of the world's great agricultural heartlands ... individuals are damaging and even killing themselves by eating too much, or too little, or alternating between these unhealthy behaviors in a pathological way."

Louis West, *Handbook of Eating Disorders*, 1987

Do you think people in rich countries who eat too much or too little care enough about those in poor countries who cannot get enough to eat?

We often eat rich fatty foods even when we are not hungry.

Why we eat

All animals are born with a control system to tell them when they need to eat, and it is this control system that makes us feel hungry. In the brain, there are two centers: a hunger center that tells us when to eat because we need energy, and a satiety center that tells us when to stop eating because we have had enough.

If we obeyed these control systems and ate only when we felt hungry and stopped as soon as we felt full, nearly all of us would consume the right amount of food for our own needs. But few of us do. We override the control systems and eat even when we are not hungry.

Top athletes consume a diet carefully tailored to their particular energy requirements.

We eat some things, such as chocolate, desserts, and french fries, because we love the taste. We have meals at set times out of habit, not necessarily because we are hungry. Often we eat food we like just because it is put in front of us.

People with eating disorders frequently override their control systems. Those with anorexia ignore hunger signals that tell them it is time to eat and those with bulimia and compulsive eating disorders take no notice of satiety signals telling them they are full.

How much food do we need?

The amount of food we need depends on how much energy we use up in a normal day. The amount of energy in food is measured in calories, and so is the energy we expend during the day. A top athlete uses up a lot of energy in training and needs to consume far more calories than an office worker who sits at a desk all day.

To stay healthy, a person should eat food containing roughly the same number of calories they use up during the day. Experts have calculated that an average teenage girl should eat foods that will give her about 2,300 calories of energy per day. An average teenage boy should take in around 2,800 calories per day.

Starchy foods such as bread, potatoes, rice, and pasta are a good source of glucose for energy, and also provide much-needed nutrients. Sweet foods such as cake and cookies can supply a lot of calories but they also contain sugar, which provides energy, but no nutrients.

Genetic programming or family lifestyle?

Some people stay slim even though they eat a lot and, conversely, others seem to put on weight very easily. Such tendencies often run in families. Overweight parents tend to have larger children, while lean parents are likely to have thinner children.

This has puzzled scientists for years. There are at least two possible reasons for these family trends. Either children inherit something from their parents in their genes that makes them prone to being fat or thin, or their weight is decided by their family's lifestyle. Overeating and too little exercise are likely to make the whole family overweight—parents and children.

This is an example of the "nature versus nurture" debate that is going on in many areas of scientific research. Just as scientists are not sure how much our weight is due to our genes (nature) and how much to our lifestyles (nurture), they are still debating whether it is our genes or the experiences and opportunities we have as we grow up that decide how we turn out as adults—physically and mentally.

Nature over nurture?

A series of studies carried out in Denmark over the last 20 years seem to support the role of nature over that of nurture. It was found that children who were adopted at birth tended to reach similar weights to their natural, not their adopted, parents. Twins were also shown to have a similar weight and build in later life, whether or not they lived together as children or were brought up in separate homes.

The "ob" gene

A few years ago, scientists became very excited when they discovered a gene in mice that made the animals fat. They called it the "ob" gene. "Ob" is short for "obesity"—the word doctors use for people who are so overweight that they are endangering their health. This is quite different from being a little overweight and needs to be taken seriously.

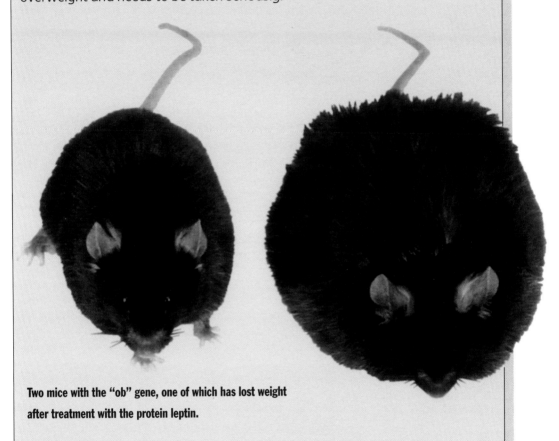

Two mice with the "ob" gene, one of which has lost weight after treatment with the protein leptin.

Animals with the "ob" gene did not make enough of a protein, called leptin, to tell their bodies when they were full. So they kept eating and became very fat. Similar "ob" genes have been found in humans but they are very rare, and most people who are overweight do not seem to have them. Researchers are still looking for other genes that might explain why some families tend to be fat and others thin. But it is quite likely that both genes and family lifestyles are important.

The body beautiful?

Talking point

"I never understood the fuss about models until I went to a fashion show and there I was totally swept away. They are indeed fabulous aliens, not like the rest of us at all ... they are never given food, they cry a lot but claim to be having the best time and, yes, they are gorgeous beyond belief."

Suzanne Moore, the *Independent*, September 18, 1998

Are rich supermodels to be envied or pitied for staying so thin?

Nine out of ten people with eating disorders are women, and many are young. Although genes may play a part in deciding why some people weigh more than others, no genes for eating disorders have been found in women or men, so other factors must be at work.

For centuries, women—and, to an extent, men—have been under pressure to conform to whatever body shape was considered to be beautiful at the time. Today, fashion and the media place pressure on women to be thin.

Many of today's supermodels are "fashionably thin" as well as being extremely beautiful. This results in the two things being linked in modern society: to be slim is to be beautiful.

Waif-like models, with blank faces and hollow eyes, are frequently shown in newspapers and fashion magazines. Young actresses and television personalities parade at parties and opening nights, their tiny bodies barely covered by even tinier dresses. In the stores, "fashionable" female clothing is cut to show off flat chests, small waists, boyish hips, and long thin legs.

Perceptions of what is "attractive" in men are increasingly being shaped by male models.

Male fashion is also more demanding than ever before. Male models, with flat stomachs and well-toned muscles, advertise desirable products to a generation of men that takes far more interest in clothes and accessories than its fathers and grandfathers ever did.

The influence of the past

Fashion has always made a lot of demands of us. Pictures of Queen Elizabeth I, at the height of her power in the late sixteenth century, show a woman whose breasts have been pressed flat against her chest by a rigid whalebone bodice. Her tiny waist is emphasized by a vast hooped skirt. Such skirts were so difficult to sit down in that special chairs had to be designed for the unfortunate wearers to use.

Even a woman as powerful as Elizabeth I of England bowed to contemporary ideas of the body beautiful.

Women endured these uncomfortable clothes because they wanted their bodies to conform to the shape that was then considered beautiful. There was no diet industry to help them count their calories and consume low-fat foods. Although people did not sit down each day to the sort of ten-course banquets often shown in historical films, the better-off did eat well, and fatty meats and dairy foods were usually on the menu. Tight bodices—and later, corsets—not only allowed women to give their bodies the shape demanded by society, but they also limited the amount of food they could physically hold in their stomachs without being sick.

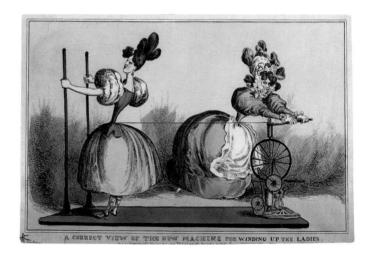

"The winding up of the ladies." A satirical cartoon highlighting the demands of women's fashion, published in 1840.

A CORRECT VIEW OF THE NEW MACHINE FOR WINDING UP THE LADIES

During some of the worst extremes of fashion in the seventeenth century, women in the poorer classes suffered least. They could not afford the sumptuous designs and materials that clothed the bodies of aristocratic women. Nor could they have performed the arduous work of running a home, bringing up a large family, and possibly working in the fields or as servants if they had worn the tight garments that upper-class fashion so often demanded.

Let nature take its course

"Why, Madam, do you know there are upward of thirty yards of bowels squeezed underneath that girdle of your daughter's? Go home and cut it; let Nature have fair play, and you will have no need of my advice."

From the memoirs of John Abernethy,
English surgeon, 1764–1831

Tight corsets once again became the fashion in the nineteenth century.

Their wardrobes contained looser, lighter, less structured versions of the clothes worn by richer women. These were more comfortable and made greater allowance for female bodies undergoing frequent pregnancy and childbirth.

In the later part of the eighteenth century, clothing for women of all social classes in Europe and America began to take on a simpler, softer, more comfortable look. Rich and poor started to dress in a similar way. But the increasing availability of fashion magazines in the nineteenth century put more pressure on women to keep up with small changes in style and cut, and the development of factories meant that garments could be produced in larger quantities and were therefore more readily available.

It wasn't long before fashionable ideas about how the female body should look meant that women were once more being laced into tight corsets to show off tiny waists under romantic, floaty dresses, with bell-shaped skirts. Little wonder that smelling salts became part of every well-dressed woman's accessories when a combination of heat and restrictive clothing sent so many swooning to the floor.

The twentieth-century body

Early in the twentieth century a minor revolution in attitudes toward women's fashion took place as a result of World War I (1914–1918). Because so many men were off fighting during the war, many European women had to take on men's jobs. It was impossible for them to work on farms and in factories in tight, restrictive clothing, and so women's clothes became more masculine in style.

In the 1920s and 1930s, fashion, rather than necessity, dictated a more "boyish" look for women that has been in and out of favor ever since. Then, as now, women's fashion made little allowance for women with larger breasts and thicker waists, and nowadays top designers demand that women fit into their tightly cut clothes without the help of sturdy underwear. They have to rely on their ability to control their food intake in order to keep their bodies in line.

The less restrictive "look" of the 1920s paved the way for modern fashion.

After the shortages and rationing of World War II (1939–1945), steadily improving living standards meant there was more to tempt a woman's appetite. Just at the time that they stopped wearing corsets and girdles to make their stomachs flat, better food meant that women were becoming heavier.

During the 1950s and 1960s people in richer countries had greater access to food than ever before. They had a more varied diet, and sweet, fatty foods—which had previously been luxuries that only the wealthiest people could afford—became widely available. The result: the average size of people in these countries began to increase.

The average twentieth-century human body continues to get bigger. A survey carried out by a mail-order clothing company found that, in the last 40 years, the female body has become rounder, with bigger, lower breasts, a larger waist, and a more pronounced stomach. The ribcage is larger and the upper arms are fuller.

Richer, tastier food, a naturally bigger body, and unforgiving clothing: this is a tough combination for today's women to deal with if they want to look and dress like the supermodels, pop singers, and actresses they see and read about.

> ## "Eating for two"
> In the West during the 1950s and 1960s, pregnant women were encouraged to "eat for two" and were congratulated on their "bouncing babies" with big fat cheeks. As many schools cut back on sports, children had less exercise but continued to eat a high-fat diet. Plump children grew into overweight adolescents and even larger adults who, in turn, had bigger babies.

San Francisco, 1950: Tim Wooster and his mother demonstrate the benefits of "eating for two."

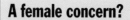

A female concern?

"The most pressing concerns of teenage girls are diet and weight. I believe this is because of the unrealistically thin bodies shown on television and in magazines. Seldom do pictures show the perfect guy who just lost five pounds in five days."

Rachel Lynne Levine, age 14,
USA Today, July 25, 1998

Some manufacturers who produce clothes for the mass market do make allowance for today's female body. But their designs must compete with those worn by the supermodels on the catwalks of New York, Paris, and Rome.

Many people feel that to look good in the latest fashions, you have to be thin. Others find it hard to control their weight and drift backward and forward between being thin and being overweight. They never establish the sort of healthy eating that will maintain their body weight at the right level for their own physical and emotional needs. Instead, they develop—and fight a continuing battle against—eating disorders.

Danish supermodel Helena Christensen at a fashion show in New York in 1997.

Case study

Lucy, a 12-year-old girl living in California, believes that she must stay thin so that she can keep up with the latest fashions. She dreads putting on weight, often a natural consequence of puberty.

"The kind of clothes I want to wear don't look good if you've got a flabby belly and big hips. I want to be able to wear hipster jeans and cut-off T-shirts, and I've got a really cool shift dress for parties, but it shows up every bulge if you put on even a few pounds. So I know I've got to be careful what I eat.

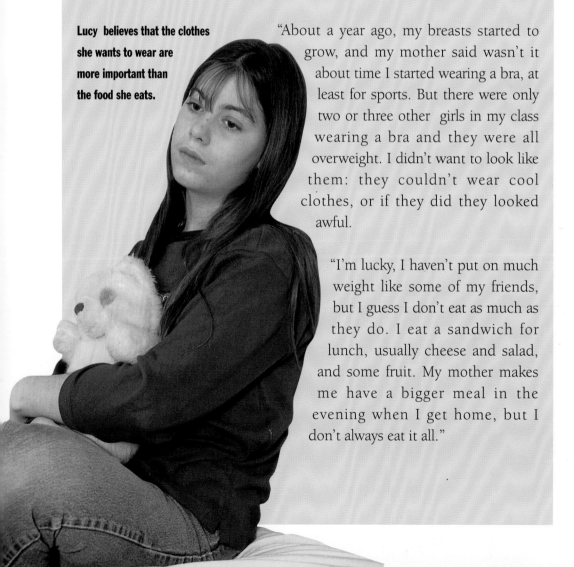

Lucy believes that the clothes she wants to wear are more important than the food she eats.

"About a year ago, my breasts started to grow, and my mother said wasn't it about time I started wearing a bra, at least for sports. But there were only two or three other girls in my class wearing a bra and they were all overweight. I didn't want to look like them: they couldn't wear cool clothes, or if they did they looked awful.

"I'm lucky, I haven't put on much weight like some of my friends, but I guess I don't eat as much as they do. I eat a sandwich for lunch, usually cheese and salad, and some fruit. My mother makes me have a bigger meal in the evening when I get home, but I don't always eat it all."

Anorexia

If you go to a European or American school of average size, there are probably between six and ten students with anorexia. It is most common in girls, but boys can also suffer from it. Anorexia tends to start around puberty, from 11–13 years of age, and most frequently occurs in people in their mid- to late teens. However, anorexia can affect children as young as five, as well as some adults.

People with anorexia worry about food all the time, and they know how many calories are in everything they eat. They are convinced that they are fat and keep trying to lose weight. When they look in the mirror they do not see their bodies as they really are. They see a much fatter person, and want to be thinner.

Men suffer too
About 5 percent of people with anorexia and bulimia are male, though among schoolchildren this may be as high as 25 percent.

Distorted self-image is common in anorexia.

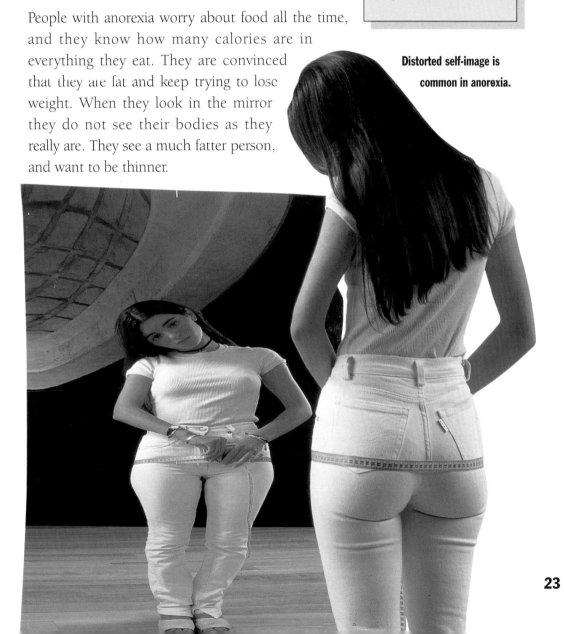

Avoiding french fries and fatty foods does not mean you have anorexia. But some people cannot stop dieting.

Many people stop eating foods that contain a lot of calories, such as candy, cookies, and cake, in order to lose weight. However, those who develop anorexia continue to "diet" long after they have reached a healthy weight.

As the condition worsens, they eat less and less, and eventually avoid eating meals altogether. Half an apple or a few potato chips may be all an anorexic will eat in a whole day. Although everyone else can see that they are becoming very thin, anorexics still see themselves as too fat, and are afraid of putting on weight if they eat more.

Some people with anorexia get a lot of exercise to help them lose weight and stay thin. At first, they seem to have lots of energy and they feel really "high." But as they become thinner, they start to feel tired and weak. They may feel depressed and sad and find it hard to concentrate. They lose interest in school, work, friends, and life in general. Everything becomes too much effort, and anorexics begin to feel that everyone is against them.

> ### Never enough
> "Even when you know you've lost weight, it's like a minute of happiness, but it's got to be more because it's never enough."
>
> Anonymous teenage girl,
> British TV show,
> September 1998

Anorexia is a very serious disease. It can kill, or do permanent damage to the body. When young people don't eat enough, they get stomach pains and constipation, feel dizzy and cold, and stop growing properly. Their bones can become brittle and break. Girls stop having periods and both sexes may become infertile. Even if their anorexia is cured, they may not be able to have children when they are older.

Lack of food can damage all the organs of the body, so that they stop working properly. If the kidneys fail, the body cannot get rid of waste products, and people need to go to the hospital several times a week to have their blood cleaned by a process known as dialysis. When the liver or heart stops working, people die.

To you, she probably looks extremely thin; to her, she is still horribly fat.

People with anorexia can become obsessed with weighing themselves after eating the tiniest meals.

Why people suffer from anorexia

There is no single cause of anorexia, and there is much debate among doctors and sociologists about the possible reasons for people becoming anorexic. Since anorexic tendencies often occur around puberty, one possible reason may be that young people are trying to stop themselves from growing up.

Girls who stay thin tend to have small breasts. Their hips stay narrow and they may not have periods. They do not have a woman's shape. Boys who do not eat properly around puberty may also delay growing up and taking on a man's shape. By not eating properly, these young people are trying to keep control of their bodies instead of letting them go through the natural changes of puberty. Some girls and boys may, knowingly or subconsciously, feel there are advantages to staying a child.

Talking point

"Anorexia reflects an ambivalence about femininity, a rebellion against feminization that in its particular form expresses both a rejection and an exaggeration of the image. The refusal of food which makes her extremely thin straightens out the girl's curves and is a denial of her essential femaleness. At the same time, this thinness parodies feminine petiteness. It is as though the anorexic has a foot in both camps—the pre-adolescent boy-girl and the young attractive woman."

Susie Orbach, *Fat Is a Feminist Issue*

What do you think are the main reasons for girls becoming anorexic?

Becoming an adult brings new responsibilities, conflicts, relationships, and decisions about what to do in life.

Some people become anorexic because they are terrified of being fat. They want to look and dress like the young people they see in magazines and on television. They want to be able to wear the fashionable clothes they see in the stores. If their friends are slim, they want to be slim too. However, people come in all shapes and sizes. Some are naturally taller, shorter, larger, or smaller than others. Some have big, strong bones and others have smaller, thinner ones. We inherit many of these characteristics from our parents, and it is quite hard to do anything about them. However, some young people are so determined to have today's popular, thin body shape that they will do anything to get it.

People come in all shapes and sizes, and most young people accept that they cannot look like models or pop stars. However, those with unreasonably high expectations of themselves and low self-esteem may develop eating disorders.

Some people use anorexia as a way of dealing with other problems. Perhaps they are lonely or shy and do not have many friends. They may be unhappy at home because their parents fight a lot or are getting divorced. They may have lots of arguments with their parents or with other members of their family. They may feel that no one cares about them at home. Not eating properly may be their way of asking for help or of showing there is something they can take charge of. When everything is going wrong around them they can at least control their weight. Or they may feel that, if they lose weight and get thinner, people will like them more and they won't feel so left out.

Loneliness and isolation are two possible situations that may cause people to consider severe dieting.

Acceptably thin?

"There were many starving girls in my junior high school, and every one was a teacher's paragon. We were allowed to come and go, racking up gold stars, as our hair fell out in fistfuls and the pads flattened behind the sockets of our eyes. When our eyeballs moved, we felt the resistance. They allowed us to haul our bones around the swinging rope in gym class, where nothing but the force of an exhausted will stood between the ceiling and the polished wooden floor thirty-five feet below."

Naomi Wolf, *The Beauty Myth*

Treating anorexia

There is no instant cure for anorexia and every case is different. Some people are so ill by the time they see a doctor that they need treatment to save their lives. They may be too ill and weak to eat and need liquid food, which is passed through a tube into the stomach. They may also need fluids, which are administered through tubes into the bloodstream.

Less serious cases do not need such desperate treatment. But people usually need help to get back into a routine of eating regular meals containing a healthy mixture of carbohydrate, fat, and protein. This can be done in a hospital or at a special unit for people with eating disorders.

Without emergency treatment, this anorexic woman could well have died.

An important element of treating anorexia is getting patients to accept that they have the illness.

Anorexia treatment works best when people want to get better and agree that they need to put on weight. At first, they may think they are eating far too much and feel full very quickly. As they start to put on weight they will worry about getting fat and will need a lot of reassurance. It is no good expecting people recovering from anorexia to put on a lot of weight right away; that would frighten them back into their dangerous eating patterns. They have to be encouraged to put on a little at a time, so that they do not see a sudden change in their appearance when they look in the mirror.

Anorexia is very hard to treat if people do not agree that they need to put on weight and continue to refuse to eat properly. Further difficulties in treatment can arise because anorexics often deny that they have the condition at all. They can become angry and defensive at the suggestion that they may be anorexic.

An anorexic receives psychotherapy counseling. The counselor makes her look at herself in a mirror in an effort to persuade her that she is not overweight.

In many countries, parents can make decisions for young people under a certain age, usually 16, and can give permission for a child to have treatment even if she or he resists. However, doctors prefer to work *with* their patients and try very hard to persuade them to cooperate, whatever their age. The older people are, the harder it becomes to treat them if they do not agree to treatment.

Case study

Mark is 13 years old. He has been treated for anorexia, but he is still very thin.

"I didn't suddenly stop eating, it just crept up on me. I was always rather chubby in junior high school and the other kids used to make fun of me because I couldn't run very fast. I was always one of the last to get picked for any team in games.

"I had a stomach bug and lost a little weight while I was sick. I was rather pleased, so I decided to eat a little less. I didn't bother much with dinner, and my mother went to evening classes and was always in such a rush she didn't really notice whether I ate.

"I hoped that if I was thinner, I would be better at sports and have more friends. But the other kids still made fun of me, because my legs got extremely thin.

"My teacher phoned my mother about my weight and she took me to the doctor. I've seen loads of specialists and, when I got very thin, they put me in the hospital. They tried to frighten me into eating by telling me I would die. In the end, I agreed to eat more so that I could come home. But as soon as

Peer pressure and self-consciousness were major factors leading to Mark's anorexia.

I started putting on weight, I panicked and went back to not eating. I have terrible fights with my father about it, and he blames my mother. I just wish they'd leave me alone. It's my body."

The support and understanding of friends and family can make a great contribution to an anorexic's recovery.

Finding out what's wrong

It is important to try to find out why someone has stopped eating. This usually means talking to the whole family, not just the person with anorexia. Parents may not realize the effect their arguments have on their family, or that one of their children is feeling unloved and left out. It may be very hard to talk about such problems and it can take many months to find out what is wrong.

People with anorexia can also have therapy to help them feel better about themselves and understand why being thin is not the answer. The therapist can help them to recognize the nice things about themselves so that they can become more confident and feel less isolated. Treatment can be carried out in one-to-one sessions with the therapist or in a group of other people with the same problem.

Long-term recovery

The aim of treatment is first to get a person to accept that he or she has the illness. After this, patients are encouraged to eat regularly and maintain a reasonable weight for long periods of time, even if they stay rather thin. However, many people relapse and stop eating properly. They need a lot of support from family and friends to help them resist the temptation to diet. A vital part of treatment is the building-up of a person's self-esteem. In this way, people can learn to care about themselves enough to take responsibility for their own nourishment.

Bulimia

Bulimia is more common than anorexia; and the number of cases is increasing rapidly. It does not usually start until people are in their late teens or early twenties and may be harder to detect than anorexia. That is because people with bulimia may not be very thin and can be very secretive about their illness. Bulimia affects many more women than men. It is just as dangerous as anorexia, and can be fatal.

People with bulimia are worried about getting too fat but they do not starve themselves. Instead, they binge on food and then make themselves vomit so that none of the food is digested or the calories are absorbed. When they binge they can eat an enormous amount of food—boxes of cookies, pies, all the cooked food in the refrigerator—as much as 15,000 calories in one to two hours.

"Bingeing" on large amounts of food: a characteristic of bulimia.

Case study

Claudette shares an apartment in Paris with her friend, Fabienne. They are both students, in their final year at the university.

"At first I thought Fabienne was really lucky. She seemed to be able to eat huge amounts of food without putting on any weight. In fact she was quite thin. Sometimes, I would hear a noise in the night and come down to find her raiding the refrigerator. There would be food all over the place. She always explained it by saying she had been so busy at college all day, she had not had time to eat, and now she was making up for it.

"Then I started to notice that, whenever we went out for a meal, she would keep going to the bathroom and be away for some time. She looked pale when she came back and would always smell of breath freshener.

"I read an article about bulimia in a magazine and I soon realized that was Fabienne's problem. But I haven't been able to get her to talk about it. I showed her the article but she just said how horrible, and that people who made themselves sick must be really weird.

"I don't know what to do. If I tell her parents or talk to one of the teachers at college I will feel disloyal. But I am worried that she is making herself really ill. I think maybe I will call the student hotline and ask what to do. You can talk to them without giving your name, so I won't feel I am letting Fabienne down."

Bingeing makes people feel physically and emotionally sick and guilty. They only feel better when they have vomited.

Some bulimics use laxatives to "hurry" food through the intestine before it is properly absorbed. But in fact, nearly all the calories are absorbed before the food has reached the part of the intestine where laxatives begin to work.

On the increase
Joint American and British research showed a threefold increase in recorded cases of bulimia between 1988 and 1994.

Fabienne keeps her bulimia secret even from her best friend.

The effects of bulimia

Bingeing on food and then vomiting, or taking laxatives to "hurry" food through the intestine, is very bad for the body. Vomiting makes the throat sore and inflamed and swallowing becomes difficult. Acid in the food brought up from the stomach damages the esophagus and may make it bleed. If the intestine is repeatedly forced to expel partly digested food, it stops working properly.

Frequent vomiting also leads to dehydration as fluids are brought up with the food. This upsets the balance of chemicals in the blood and makes people dizzy and confused. It can even make the heart stop. People who vomit a lot tend to have bad breath and all the acid in their mouth makes their teeth decay. The glands in the neck become enlarged and the skin gets dry. Taking lots of laxatives is very bad for the intestines. They lose their protective lining and become inflamed and prone to infection.

Frequent vomiting leads to dehydration, and in some cases can cause throat rupture.

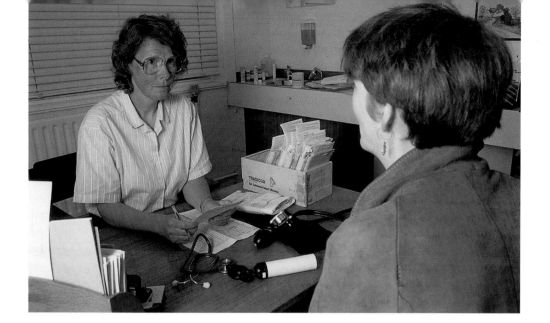

The faster bulimia is treated, the easier it is to cure. Most people need expert help to break the cycle of the illness.

Why people become bulimic

Since bulimia usually starts after puberty, it seems unlikely that people binge and vomit to delay growing up. But bulimia can result from the same pressures to be fashionably thin that lead to anorexia. People who diet in order to increase their self-esteem may also develop bulimia.

Bulimia is frequently a way of coping with unhappiness. Many people with bulimia seem to be happy and successful. They may have lots of friends and plenty to do. But deep inside, they feel scared, helpless, and worthless. Bingeing and vomiting is the only way they know to relieve their distress.

Treating bulimia

Unlike people with anorexia, who often will not accept that they have a problem, those with bulimia usually know they are ill. However, it may be years before they seek help. During treatment, bulimics learn to stop worrying so much about their weight and body shape and to establish a more healthy pattern of eating.

37

Bulimia traps its sufferers in a vicious cycle. Anxieties and unhappiness are alleviated by bingeing. Guilt immediately follows, and bulimics see "purging" themselves of the food they have just eaten as a "quick fix" to get rid of their guilt. Because of this, treatment often includes "deprogramming" the urge to vomit after a session of overeating and relaxation therapy to reduce anxiety.

Diana, Princess of Wales, whose bulimia was an expression of her deep unhappiness.

Talking point

"It was a symptom of what was going on in my marriage. I was crying out for help, but giving the wrong signals, and people were using my bulimia as a coat on a hanger: they decided that was the problem—Diana was unstable."

Diana, Princess of Wales, *Panorama*, BBC TV, November 1995

Diana felt that people were ignoring the underlying causes of her distress. Why do you think this happened?

Compulsive eating

Some people eat huge amounts of food but, unlike those with bulimia, they do not try to get rid of it by vomiting or using laxatives. They are known as compulsive eaters, and they ignore the body's natural signals, which tell them when they need to eat. This means that they eat when they are not hungry and go on eating long after they feel full.

Like people with bulimia, compulsive eaters tend to consume large amounts of sweet, fatty, high-calorie foods, and they have many of the same emotional problems as bulimia sufferers. They eat too much because they are unhappy or depressed. They may feel unloved and inadequate. Eating a lot, usually in secret, is their way of coping with their misery. However, far from making people feel better, compulsive eating tends to make them feel embarrassed and worthless because they cannot control their eating.

Talking point

"A curious aspect in the compulsive eater's addiction is that from a look at her kitchen or her public eating one might get the impression that certain foods are illegal. The presence of certain foods is so rare, and ingestion so clandestine, that one might be forgiven for assuming that criminal penalties are given for the possession and consumption of certain foods."

Susie Orbach,
Fat Is a Feminist Issue

Should compulsive eaters be made to feel wicked if they have cake and cookies? Or would a more relaxed approach help them deal with their problem and eat normally?

Compulsive eaters overeat and then diet or starve to try to avoid putting on weight.

Since they do not burn all the extra calories from their bodies, many compulsive eaters are overweight. Up to 40 percent of the people who are obese may also be compulsive eaters. They go on frequent diets to get thinner, but put the weight back on when they return to their unhealthy eating habits.

Compulsive eating is bad for the body. Consuming large amounts of sugary foods results in swings in blood sugar. This can make people feel irritable and tired. They will crave more sugar, no matter how much has already been eaten. The result is more compulsive eating.

Ironically, many compulsive eaters are malnourished because their craving for sweet foods means that they do not eat enough nutritious food. If serious weight problems develop as a result of compulsive eating, there is a danger of developing diabetes, heart and artery disease, joint problems, and even cancer.

Why people become compulsive eaters

Compulsive eating can start at any time in life, but often begins during the teenage years. Problems at school or at home can make young people feel isolated and unhappy, and they turn to food to make them feel better. Most of us have used "comfort food" to get over some disappointment, but some compulsive eaters use food to try to get over a much deeper unhappiness that never really goes away.

> ## The trap of obsession
>
> "My day revolves around food. I tell myself: 'I'll eat good today. Today, I'm going to do better, start to lose some weight, exercise, etc.' And then later in the day at some inevitable point, I binge. Guilt follows, and I want to die. I realize that I have a problem, even though I never purge or starve myself ... I am afraid to make friends, have relationships with men, etc., because I am worried that they will judge me and think I am too fat, flabby, and repulsive to consider."
>
> Jennifer, contributor to the Eating Disorders Association website, Australia, May 1998

Compulsive eating patterns often begin during the teenage years.

Case study

Hannah was bullied at junior high school by two other girls in her class who made her life miserable. Now, at 14, she eats whenever she feels unhappy and then feels bad when she gets on the scales and weighs herself.

"I don't know why, but wherever I go, I'm the one who gets picked on by the other kids. I try to fit in and make friends, but I'm no good at sports and I don't find it easy to talk to new people. I don't know what to say, so I just stand around, and kids think I'm stuck up.

"When I get home, my parents are at work, so I just go up to my room with some bags of potato chips and candy or a big tub of popcorn that I buy on the way home from school. I listen to CDs and stuff my face with food until it's time for supper. My mother's a really good cook, so I have no problem eating at mealtimes as well.

Unhappy at home and at school, Hannah resorts to food for comfort.

"I used to get away with eating so much and didn't seem to put on weight. But now I'm older, I know I'm getting fat. I tried going on a diet but it didn't work because something horrible happened at school and I bought a huge bar of chocolate and it started all over again."

Unfortunately, the opportunities for compulsive eating in some countries, particularly the United States, and increasingly in Europe, are greater than ever before. With hamburgers and doughnuts available in every shopping mall, and supermarkets packed with convenience foods available around the clock, it is very easy to eat at any time of the day or night. The days when people ate three times a day—breakfast, lunch and dinner—are long gone, and it is easy to snack almost from the moment you wake up.

Treating compulsive eating

Compulsive eating disorder does not respond well to psychotherapy or general counseling. Instead, a program of "reeducation" is often used. Compulsive eaters need to control their negative thoughts about food and eating and to rebuild their self-esteem.

This requires the professional help of doctors and therapists. Some compulsive eaters may also benefit from the advice of a dietitian. Dietitians can help them plan regular meals that will provide the energy and nutrition they need, without excessive amounts of fat and sugar.

Dieting and obesity

The diet industry is worth an estimated $33 billion in the United States alone. Every day, around the world, millions of people start diets, buy dieting books, or begin punishing exercise regimes in an effort to lose weight. Since so few of these programs actually work, there is a constant demand for new and different diets, and those who work in the weight-loss business can make a lot of money.

The ever-increasing popularity of gyms and health clubs reflects people's concerns about their fitness and their weight.

Diets rarely, if ever, work in isolation, and dieters often regain the weight they lost as soon as they begin to eat normally again.

A 50 percent increase

The 1998 Health Survey for England showed that 61 percent of men and 52 percent of women are overweight. Of these, 16 percent of men and 18 percent of women are clinically obese. This is an increase of almost 50 percent since 1988.

Some people manage to lose weight when they go on a diet, but when they start eating normally again they soon put back all the weight they had lost, and sometimes more. This is very depressing and can lead to eating disorders such as anorexia, bulimia, and compulsive eating.

Experts agree that the best way to stay the right weight for your height is to eat a healthy, balanced diet all the time. That means a mixture of foods containing all the nutrients the body needs. People who eat a healthy, balanced diet when they are young are less likely to have weight problems when they are older. They set a pattern of eating that they can follow all their lives.

People who develop the habit of healthy eating when they are young will usually maintain it throughout their lives.

Why diet?

Most people diet because they think they are overweight. But are they? In a recent 1998 survey, half of the young women taking part who were a healthy weight wanted to be thinner. Nearly 60 percent of them felt guilty about eating certain foods, usually chocolate, cake, and french fries. Yet they weighed an amount widely considered to be right for their height and build.

A vicious circle

"When the front pages call you the Duchess of Pork, it makes you lose all your self-esteem and self-confidence and you eat more because of the emotional upset that you are feeling. So the whirlwind keeps spiraling on until you get to Weight Watchers, where you don't have to deny yourself anything, including wine, which therefore means that at last you are taking control of your weight."

Sarah, Duchess of York, Weight Watchers website, January 1998

Much of the pressure to lose weight and avoid certain foods comes from the media, but it also comes from those around us. From an early age, we learn that buying candy and cake is somehow wrong. Eating a chocolate bar or a bag of potato chips is hugely pleasurable but, in the background, there are guilty feelings too.

The guilt factor: even people who are a healthy weight for their height and age can feel guilty about eating fattening foods like chocolate.

Changing trends in the way our food is made and packaged have had both positive and negative effects. Manufacturers have developed low-fat versions of many of our favorite foods, so that those who are trying to lose weight or control their weight can still eat well. But these have also helped to reinforce the guilt we associate with eating sweet, fatty things.

Most food labels now list the ingredients and the calorie content. This should make it easier for us to find out exactly what we are eating. However, food labeling can be misleading and create the illusion that a product is a "health food," when in fact it is not. For example, a food may be labeled "fat free" and still contain a large amount of sugar. Likewise, a low calorie count does not necessarily mean that a food is "healthy."

In an attempt to eat less, some people resort to taking vitamin pills instead of eating healthy food, mistakenly believing that vitamins, not nutrition, are all a body needs to function properly.

Many doctors are concerned about the growing number of people who are so overweight that they are endangering their health. But others argue that we also need to be more accepting of our weight, our shape, and the way we are and not be so critical if we weigh a few pounds more than the textbooks say we should.

Case study

Anna is 30 and works in an office. She is a little overweight but nowhere near obese. Having tried lots of different diets, she has finally decided to stop worrying about her weight.

"I think I must have tried every diet there is. Low fat, low sugar, all fruit, high protein, I've been on them all. I usually lost some weight but never as much as I wanted, and within a few months I had put it all back again.

"My big problem is chocolate. I find it really hard to go more than a day without something chocolate—candy, cookies, puddings, ice cream. When I was on a diet, I managed to stop eating chocolate, but as soon as I ended the diet, I just couldn't resist the craving.

"I know I'm not hugely overweight, but I used to get very depressed when I couldn't buy the sort of clothes I liked. They simply didn't go up to my size. It was as if the manufacturers were saying: 'You're too fat, you won't look nice in our clothes.'

"Well, at last, I've decided they can keep their clothes. I'm still careful about what I eat, but I don't diet any more. I don't feel horribly guilty if I have a chocolate bar. I just enjoy it and have an apple or banana the next day when I feel like a snack.

A false doctrine

"We've been taught to despise bulges, stretch marks, and wrinkles, in other words, all the signs of how we've lived and loved life: how we've raised kids; enjoyed good meals, a drink, and a laugh; suffered, shrugged, and moved on. That has to change."

Anita Roddick, founder of The Body Shop

"At mealtimes, I choose lean meat or fish dishes and make sure I have some salad or vegetables. I have french fries when I feel like it, and I have a dessert if I want one, but not every day.

"Over the last year, my weight has stayed very much the same. By not dieting, I haven't put on lots of weight and I no longer get on the scales each morning, terrified that I've put on a pound or two. In fact, I don't weigh myself very often. I just get on with enjoying life!"

Having stopped worrying about her weight, Anna has found that a healthy weight is not hard to maintain.

Obesity

Obesity is a word that is often misused. Many people think they or someone they know is obese when, in reality, that person is just a little overweight.

Doctors define obesity as a dangerous health problem that occurs in people whose body mass index (BMI) is over 30. BMI is a measure of body size that takes account of height as well as weight. A high BMI means that your weight is too high, whether you are tall or short. Obese people are not just a little overweight. They are so much heavier than they should be that they are making themselves ill.

More harm than good?

"While we have to examine critically the risks of obesity, we should look equally critically at the risks associated with its management.... In recommending weight loss to our patients, there is a possibility that we may sometimes do more harm than good."

Dr. William Jeffcoate, the *Lancet*, March 21, 1998

Obesity can become a great danger to health, and the condition requires regular monitoring and treatment by health professionals.

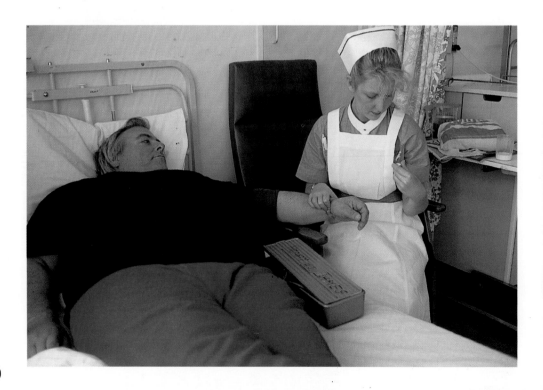

About 15–20 percent of middle-aged people in Europe and at least one out of three Americans are obese. Among some American Indians and in certain Pacific islands, up to 80 percent of the people are obese. In contrast, the figure in China is only about 1 to 2 percent, largely because the majority of Chinese people have less access to the types or amounts of food that can cause obesity.

In the United States, obesity is increasingly common.

All over the world, however, the number of people who are obese and the number who are overweight is increasing. In the UK, for example, average weight has risen by about 2.2 lbs. (1 kg) in the last 10 years, and the proportion of people who are obese has increased to over 15 percent.

The people who are most likely to be obese in richer countries, such as the United States, Europe, and Australia, are quite different from those who are at greatest risk in poorer countries such as Africa and South America.

In better-off countries a healthy lifestyle is more accessible to the wealthy than to the poor.

In the better-off countries, it is the poorest people who tend to be obese or overweight. That is probably because they cannot afford to eat a balanced diet, with a mixture of carbohydrate, fat, protein foods, fruit, and vegetables. Instead, they tend to fill up on cheap, poor-quality, sweet and fatty foods.

51

In contrast, richer people have the money to buy low-fat and low-sugar foods, and a wider range of fruit and vegetables. They can afford to go to gyms and health clubs and get plenty of exercise to keep their weight down. Better-off people also tend to have better access to information about the importance of a healthy lifestyle.

In poorer countries, such as India, it is the wealthy who are prone to eating-related health problems, because eating well is a status symbol.

In poor countries, only the wealthier people can afford a lot of food. Eating well and being overweight are seen as status symbols—they mean you are successful. Far from worrying about their weight, richer people are only too happy to show that they have plenty of money for food. As a result, wealthy people in poor countries are starting to have the same illnesses—such as heart disease, high blood pressure, and diabetes—that are seen in richer countries.

Poor people in poor countries tend to be thin. They simply cannot afford enough food to maintain a healthy weight. They have a simple diet, usually based on rice or cereal crops. Since they cannot afford foods containing protein, such as meat and fish, their children do not grow properly. Both adults and children have diseases caused by vitamin and mineral deficiencies because they do not get enough fruit and vegetables.

The future

In any discussion about how to reduce the problem of eating disorders, we should consider the things that can realistically be modified and those that are unlikely to change.

Food is an essential component of everyday life. It not only keeps us alive and healthy, but it is also a major element of some of our social rituals. In many families, mealtimes are the only time when everyone sits down together and parents and children find out what is going on in each other's lives.

Eating out is an increasingly common social activity —at the homes of friends and family or in restaurants. People are becoming more demanding about the range and complexity of the meals they eat. You cannot go into a bookstore or turn on the television without coming across new fads in cooking techniques, ingredients, or recipes. The market for cookbooks has never been greater; everyone—from actresses to politicians, princesses to paupers—seems to be involved in discovering new dishes and different ways of presenting them.

Food remains the focus for many family and cultural rituals.

This international fascination with food and the way it is grown, cooked, presented, and eaten is unlikely to go away. But if fascination with food turns into obsession about eating, there is clearly a need for change.

Discrimination

Large people frequently feel badly treated because of their size. Deliberately or without thinking, many people treat those who are overweight differently from those who weigh an average amount.

Overweight children may be teased or bullied because of their size. Their weight may make it difficult for them to be good at sports. Since they are physically slow, some people assume they are mentally slow as well. Some children simply do not want to be seen playing with someone who looks different. So overweight children can become isolated and lonely.

Adults also treat overweight people differently. Some assume overweight people are lazy, stupid, or even dirty and do not want to employ them or form relationships with them. Such discrimination is clearly unacceptable, but only through a change in social attitudes can it be stopped.

Overweight children have always been a target for bullying.

If we could treat people without regard to whether they are fat or thin, there would be less need to be a particular size or shape. If weight played no part at job interviews, people would be employed according to their ability to do the work. And if we did not worry about appearance, most of us would make friends with people who liked doing the same things we do and had the same interests and similar attitudes to life.

Feeling comfortable about their weight can be an important factor in people's enjoyment of their lives.

Role models

It is human nature to want to be like the people we admire. These people, called "role models," may be athletes, pop singers, actors, even politicians. With the same skills, hard work, and a lot of luck, some people can do similar jobs and have similar lifestyles to those of their heroes. But others can't. As we get older, most of us become more confident in our own skills and abilities, and we understand that these are very different from those of our earlier role models.

Most role models can have a very good effect on our lives, even if we end up doing something completely different. Role models can give people ideas about the way they want to live and the goals they need to set themselves, in their social and personal as well as their working lives.

The Spice Girls were important role models for many young people in the 1990s.

The desirable option?

"Not many people have actually said to me that they've looked at my magazine and decided to become anorexic or to diet so much they become anorexic. ... In a world where more and more people are finding it unpleasantly easy to be overweight because you can buy so much junk food so easily and cheaply, it becomes more desirable to be thinner than fatter. It's just a very straightforward sociological fact."

Alexandra Shulman, editor of *Vogue*, September 4, 1998

Some role models, however, can be dangerous. Sometimes the desire to look like one of today's top fashion models can result in a person's developing anorexia or bulimia. There is growing pressure on leading fashion designers to stop demanding that their models be excessively thin and to make clothes that fit real women, with average bust, waist, and hip sizes.

A widening gap
Twenty-five years ago, fashion models weighed 8 percent less than the average woman. Today, they weigh 23 percent less.

"Fashionably thin" models may have become dangerous role models for today's young women.

Talking point
"The worship of the willowy supermodel has become a cult, and the parent of even the scrawniest six-year-old girl will know that she is quite likely to come home from school announcing that she is starting a diet. Such food denial is clearly an abnormal process, and one that is in conflict with the deeply ingrained eating-oriented habits of families and societies."

Dr. William Jeffcoate, the *Lancet*, March 21, 1998

How can we encourage future generations to eat healthily?

Some designers have taken steps to employ healthier-looking models. But others insist that a young woman whose ribs and shoulder blades are clearly visible through her skin is not excessively thin. Yet, until these role models who appear daily in magazines and on television reject the emaciated look, many young women will continue to starve themselves in an effort to copy their apparent success.

Better support for young people

If young people are using anorexia, bulimia, or compulsive eating as ways to cope with life, then alternatives must be found to help them deal with difficult situations. The best way of working out day-to-day problems is to talk about them with someone else. At the very least, this provides a sympathetic ear and a shoulder to cry on and, at best, practical suggestions may be made for sorting things out.

Family and friends are one option, and trained counselors are another. Some people prefer to talk about their problems to someone they do not know, either face to face or on the telephone. There are numerous organizations in the United States and the UK that run hotlines designed for young people, including some that specialize in helping people with eating disorders (see "Useful addresses" on page 63).

Eating disorders are among the most obvious cries for help, but is anyone listening?

It is important to recognize when life may be particularly difficult for young people. A death in the family, divorce, moving house, the birth of a brother or sister are all times when it is quite common to feel anxious, depressed, or left out. .

Puberty is another time when young people can feel confused and unable to cope. The hormonal and physical changes that occur at this time can have a big effect on how you feel. Changing schools and the need to make new friends can make life even more stressful.

People who develop eating disorders to cope with problems like these speak of the shame and embarrassment they feel. Despite this, recognizing that there is a problem is the first step to recovery. Getting help is the second.

Starving yourself or overeating are two of the most obvious cries for help, their effects all too apparent. But conditions like anorexia, bulimia, and compulsive eating disorder are frequently ignored until it is almost too late to do anything about them. The long-term physical and emotional damage caused by eating disorders is well known. The aim must now be to tackle the underlying reasons why so many young women and men are using an unhealthy attitude toward food as their way of coping with the stresses and strains of modern living.

Ideally, the enjoyment of food should act as a relief from the pressures of modern life and need not lead to eating disorders.

Glossary

Artery A blood vessel that carries blood away from the heart and around the body.

Biochemical (metabolic) reactions A complex sequence of reactions involved in the digestion of food, the use of energy, and the manufacture of new body tissues.

Calorie A unit used to measure energy.

Carbohydrate One of a group of chemical compounds containing carbon, hydrogen, and oxygen. Examples are sugars and starch. Carbohydrates are the main source of food energy for animals.

Cell The smallest living part of any living thing. All the organs and other parts of the body are made up of cells.

Diabetes A hormonal disease, common in overweight people but also suffered by others. It is caused when the pancreas does not work properly so that too much sugar gets into the bloodstream.

DNA An abbreviation of deoxyribonucleic acid, which carries genetic information in chromosomes.

Energy Power required to perform some activity. The body takes energy from food and converts it into chemicals it can use to power everyday activities, such as breathing, moving, thinking, and eating.

Esophagus The tube that carries food and liquids from the mouth to the stomach.

Gene A piece of DNA inherited from one or both parents that tells the body which proteins to make. By deciding which proteins are made, genes play an important role in how we look, think, and move around, and the diseases we suffer from.

Glucose A simple sugar, which is the body's major source of energy.

Glycogen A carbohydrate used to store energy, mainly in the liver and muscles.

Heart attack A blockage of the blood flow to the heart, often leading to permanent damage to the organ.

Immune system White blood cells involved in protecting the body from invading microorganisms, such as bacteria and viruses.

Infertile Unable to have children.

Intestine The long tube in the abdomen where food is digested.

Kidney An organ of the body that processes waste products into urine and controls blood pressure.

Malnutrition Condition resulting from the lack of foods necessary for health.

Obese People are considered to be obese when they are 25 percent above the weight considered normal for their height.

Protein An important component of food. Protein is needed for growth and repair of muscles and body organs. Proteins can also be made by the body.

Psychotherapy A method of treatment for disorders of the mind. Psychotherapy aims to help self-understanding and personal development via the relationship between the patient and the therapist.

Self-esteem A good opinion of oneself.

Starch A carbohydrate found in cereals, pasta, rice, bread, and vegetables. Starch is a source of energy.

Stroke A serious illness caused when the blood supply to parts of the brain is blocked. Strokes can lead to paralysis.

Books to read

Bode, Janet. *Food Fight: A Guide to Eating Disorders for Pre-Teens and Their Parents*. New York: Simon & Schuster, 1997.

Erlanger, Ellen. *Eating Disorders: A Question and Answer Book about Anorexia Nervosa and Bulimia Nervosa*. Minneapolis, MN: Lerner Publications, 1988.

Maloney, Michael and Rachel Kranz. *Straight Talk About Eating Disorders* (Straight Talk). New York: Facts on File, 1991.

Patterson, Charles. *Eating Disorders* (Teen Hotline). Austin, TX: Raintree Steck-Vaughn, 1995.

Robbins, Paul R. *Anorexia and Bulimia* (Diseases and People). Springfield, NJ: Enslow Publications, 1998.

Sources

The Beauty Myth by Naomi Wolf. New York: Anchor, 1992.

Families and How to Survive Them by Robin Skynner and John Cleese. New York: Oxford University Press, 1984.

Fat Is a Feminist Issue by Susie Orbach. New York: Berkeley Publishing Group, 1991.

Useful addresses

American Anorexia/Bulimia
Association Inc.
165 West 46th Street #1108
New York, NY 10036
212 575 6200

Massachusetts Eating Disorders
Association
92 Pearl Street
Newton, MA 02458
617 558 1881

Overeaters Anonymous, Inc.
World Service Office (WSO)
6075 Zenith Ct. NE
Rio Rancho, NM 87124
505 891 2664

Websites

Yahoo's eating disorders links:
www.yahoo.com/Health/Mental
Health/Diseases- and Conditions/
Eating Disorders/

Infoseek's eating disorders links:
http://guide-p.infoseek.com/
Health/Mental health/Eating
disorders/

Mirror Mirror website on eating
disorders:
www.mirror-mirror.org/eatdis.htm

Eating disorders shared awareness:
http://www.eating-disorder.com/

Index

Numbers in **bold** refer to illustrations.

anorexia 5, 7, **7**, 11, 23–32
anxiety 37–38

beauty 14–22
bingeing 33, **33**, 38
biochemical reactions 8
blood vessels 9, **9**
body
    and anorexia 23, **23**, 24, 27
    average body size 20
    beauty and 14–22
body mass index (BMI) 50
bulimia 7, 11, 33–38

calories 11
causes of eating disorders 26–28, 37, 40–42
children, overweight 20, 54, **54**
China 51
Christensen, Helena **21**
compulsive eating 7, 11, 39–42
consent to treatment 30
control systems 10–11
counseling 30, **30**, 58

dehydration 36
Diana, Princess of Wales **38**
diet industry 43
dietitians 42
dieting 23–24, 43–49
discrimination 54–55

Elizabeth I, Queen of England 16, **16**
energy 8–9
    and food needed 11–12
    loss of in anorexia 24
Europe 51
exercise 43, **43**, 52

family 32
    lifestyle 12–13
fashion 14–22
    history 16–20
    models 14–15, 14, 15, 21, **21**, 57, **57**
fatty deposits 9, **9**
food 4
    amount needed 11–12
    availability 42, **42**
    quality and obesity 51–52
    social importance 53–54
    trends 17, 19–20, 46–47
    why we need it 8–9
food labeling 47

genes 12–13
glucose 8, 40
glycogen 8
guilt **10**, 38, 46–47

health problems 52
    from eating disorders 25, 35–36, 40
    from being overweight **5**, 9, 40
"health foods" 47
healthy diet **4**, 29–30, 45, **45**
hunger center 10

India **52**
intestines 35, 36

laxatives 34, 36
leptin 13
lifestyle 12–13, 52

models 14–15, **14**, **15**, 21, **21**, 57, **57**

"ob" gene 13
obesity 13, 40, 44, 50–52
organ damage 25
Owen, Michael **11**

peer pressure 27, 31, 54
poor countries 52, **52**
poverty 17–18, 51, 52
pregnancy 20
puberty 23, 26–27, 59
reeducation 42
relaxation therapy 38
rich countries 51–52, **51**
role models 55–57

satiety center 10
self-acceptance 48–49
self-esteem 32, 39, 42, 46
Spice Girls 56
sugar 12, 40
support 32, 58–59

talking over problems 58–59
therapy 30, 32, 38
thinness 14–15, 21, 27
treatment of eating disorders 29–32, 37–38, 42

unhappiness 28, 32, 37–38, **38**, 39, 40, 41
UK 5, 44, 51
United States 5, 51, **51**

vitamin pills **47**
vomiting 34, 35–36, **36**, 38

wealth 51–52, **51**, **52**
weight, average 51
westernization 6

© Copyright 1999 Wayland (Publishers) Ltd.